DATE DUE

7-21-14			

Food Chains and Webs

SCHOOL OF EDUCATION
CURRICULUM LABORATORY
UM-DEARBORN

Andrew Solway

Chicago, Illinois

www.capstonepub.com
Visit our website to find out more information about Heinemann-Raintree books.

To order:

☎ Phone 888-454-2279
💻 Visit www.capstonepub.com
to browse our catalog and order online.

Edited by Andrew Farrow, Adrian Vigliano, and Diyan Leake
Designed by Victoria Allen
Picture research by Elizabeth Alexander
Illustrations by Oxford Designers & Illustrators
Originated by Capstone Global Library Ltd
Printed and bound in China by South China Printing Company Ltd

15 14 13 12 11
10 9 8 7 6 5 4 3 2 1

Library of Congress Cataloging-in-Publication Data
Solway, Andrew.

Food chains and webs / Andrew Solway.—1st ed.

p. cm.—(The web of life)

Includes bibliographical references and index.

ISBN 978-1-4109-4397-2 (hb (freestyle))—ISBN 978-1-4109-4404-7 (pb (freestyle)) 1. Food chains (Ecology)—Juvenile literature. I. Title.

QH541.14.S668 2012

577'.16—dc23   2011017698

Acknowledgements
The author and publishers are grateful to the following for permission to reproduce copyright material: Getty Images pp. 32 (Flip Nicklin/Minden Pictures), 34 (Brian J. Skerry/National Geographic), 39 (Tom Brakefield/Digital Vision); Photolibrary pp. 5 (Malcolm Schuyl), 7 (Martin Harvey), 10 (Manfred Kage), 11 (Brigitte Thomas), 12 (Kidd Geoff), 13 (Nick Garbutt), 14 (Doug Perrine), 23 (Roberta Olenick), 37 (Richard Herrmann), 40 (Jacques Rosès), 41 (Mike Lane); Science Photo Library p. 28 (Edward Kinsman); Shutterstock pp. 8 (© Pixeldom), 16 (© hunta), 17 (© Monkey Business Images), 19 (© worldswildlifewonders), 21 (© 12qwerty), 24 (© Gregory Gerber), 27 (© Mogens Trolle), 29 (© Joy Stein), 31 (© Matthijs Wetterauw).

Cover photograph of a male cheetah with impala prey. Masai Mara, Kenya, East Africa reproduced with permission of Photolibrary (Fritz Polking/Peter Arnold Images).

Every effort has been made to contact copyright holders of material reproduced in this book. Any omissions will be rectified in subsequent printings if notice is given to the publisher.

Contents

Some words appear in the text in bold, **like this**. You can find out what they mean by looking in the glossary.

Making the Connections

Living things need food to stay alive. That is simple and obvious. But if you start looking at what food different **organisms** need, and how they get it, it all gets complicated very fast.

Food connections

For many years, scientists have been studying how living things get food. They have found that food connects living things in many different ways. For example, if animal A eats another animal B, then the two **species** are connected. But animal A is also connected to the food that animal B eats—for example, plant C. If C is in short supply, there may be fewer of species B for animal A to eat.

That's not all. Suppose animal A also eats two other kinds of animals, D and E. So if the numbers of species B are low, animal A may eat more of C and D. Species B, C, and D have a food connection through animal A. And this is only the beginning of the complications!

Connections such as these link different species together in **food chains** and **food webs**. In this book you can learn more about food chains and webs. In the process, you can find out what aliens, rotters, and pyramids have to do with feeding relationships. There's plenty of food for thought!

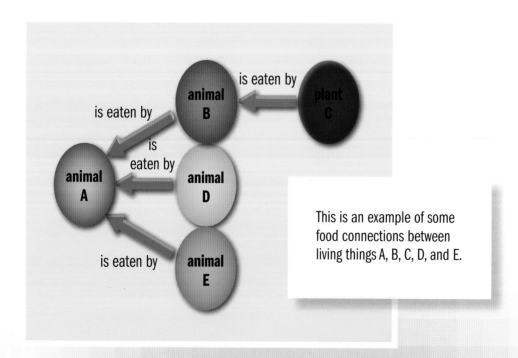

This is an example of some food connections between living things A, B, C, D, and E.

WHAT IT MEANS FOR US

Bumblebees and other wild bees are important to human food crops because they **pollinate** many plants (help them to reproduce by carrying pollen from plant to plant). In recent years the numbers of these bees have fallen, but the reasons for this are not clear.

In Europe, research has shown there are far fewer wild flowers on farms than there were in the past. These flowers are an important food source for bumblebees, so perhaps this is why bee numbers have dropped. However, in North America, the reasons may be different. A recent study suggests that North American bees may have a weakness in their **genes** that makes them prone to disease. There is also research that suggest that a pesticide called clothianide might be killing the bees.

There are more plant-eaters in the world than animals that eat other animals. Why is this? Find out on page 16.

WORD BANK

food chain   group of organisms that are connected through what they eat

food web   group of organisms that are connected through feeding relationships in

Energy

All living things need energy. Animals need energy to grow, to move around, and to keep their bodies working (for example, pumping blood around the body). Plants need energy to grow and to produce flowers, fruit, and seeds. Where does this energy come from?

A furnace in space

Plants take their energy from sunlight. The sun is a huge furnace in space, releasing incredible amounts of energy. Plants are able to capture some of this energy. They use it to combine two very simple substances—**carbon dioxide (CO_2)** and water—to make more complex chemicals such as sugars and **starch**.

Sugars and starch are chemicals that have energy stored in them. If a plant breaks these chemicals back down to CO_2 and water, the energy is released. So whenever the plant needs energy, it can get it by breaking down sugars or starch. They are the plant's food.

This diagram shows how the sun supplies nearly all the energy on Earth.

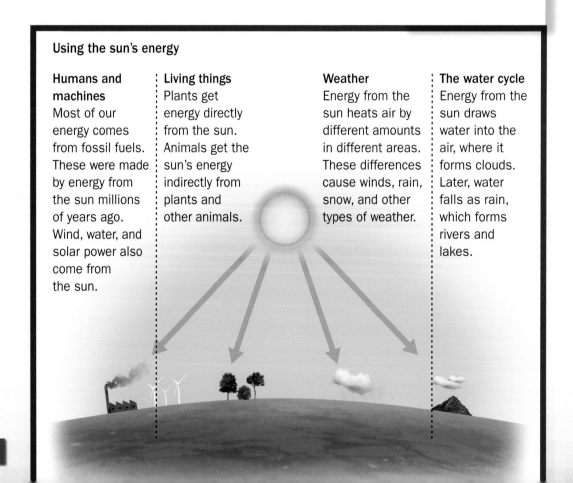

Using the sun's energy

Humans and machines	Living things	Weather	The water cycle
Most of our energy comes from fossil fuels. These were made by energy from the sun millions of years ago. Wind, water, and solar power also come from the sun.	Plants get energy directly from the sun. Animals get the sun's energy indirectly from plants and other animals.	Energy from the sun heats air by different amounts in different areas. These differences cause winds, rain, snow, and other types of weather.	Energy from the sun draws water into the air, where it forms clouds. Later, water falls as rain, which forms rivers and lakes.

Endotherms and ectotherms

Different living things need different amounts of energy just to stay alive. Animals, such as mammals and birds, are **endothermic**. They generate heat inside their bodies to keep them at a constant, fairly high temperature. By contrast, many lizards, snakes, and frogs are ectothermic. They warm their bodies by soaking up heat from the environment (for example, by basking in the sun). Ectotherms need less energy to stay alive because they don't keep their bodies at a constant temperature.

A gazelle like this will feed a lion for several days. However, an ectotherm such as a snake could live for weeks on a similar meal, because it needs far less energy.

High-energy animals

Hummingbirds use more energy than any other type of animal. They eat their own body weight in food every day. Hummingbirds need to feed every 15 to 20 minutes to keep their energy levels high. If they cannot feed, they go into a kind of "suspended animation" called torpor, where their energy use drops dramatically. Their body temperature drops when they are resting.

In a similar way, a bat allows its body temperature to fall when **hibernating**, in order to save energy.

Common confusions

What do we mean by "animals"?

When we talk about "animals" we usually mean furry or hairy animals, such as dogs, cats, lions, bears, or apes. These are all mammals. However, in science, the word *animal* means much more than this. The animal kingdom includes sponges, several kinds of worms, spiders, insects, fish, amphibians (frogs and newts), reptiles (lizards, turtles, and crocodiles), and birds, as well as mammals.

WORD BANK
endothermic produces heat within the body to keep temperature constant no matter how the temperature of the environment changes
ectothermic needs to get heat from the surroundings to keep warm

Producers

A producer, or a primary producer, is any living thing that can make its own food. The majority of producers on Earth make their food by **photosynthesis**.

Scrubland is the kind of vegetation that grows in many parts of the Mediterranean. It is sometimes called maquis.

Producers on land

On land, plants are the main producers. Wherever they can get enough water and light, and the temperature is not too cold, plants cover the Earth's surface. Forests grow where there is enough rainfall to supply the trees with water. Drier areas are mainly covered by grasses, **scrubland** plants, or desert plants such as cacti.

Plants need **carbon dioxide (CO_2)** from the air, and water (usually from the soil) to photosynthesize. They also need small amounts of simple chemicals such as nitrates (substances containing nitrogen) and phosphates (substances containing phosphorus). These **nutrients** are usually dissolved in water from the soil, and plants can get enough to survive simply by taking in water.

Food factories

Leaves are the main food factories of green plants. Leaves are thin and flat, so that as much of the leaf as possible gets sunlight. Their stems can twist slowly, so that the top surface stays facing the sun. The top part of every leaf is packed with **cells** that are specialized for photosynthesis. The green color in leaves is a pigment (colored chemical) called **chlorophyll**. This is the substance that actually captures energy from the sun. The energy is used to make sugars from CO_2 and water.

One important waste product of photosynthesis is oxygen. Without oxygen, animals could not get energy from their food. So, as well as producing food for us to eat, plants produce oxygen for us to breathe.

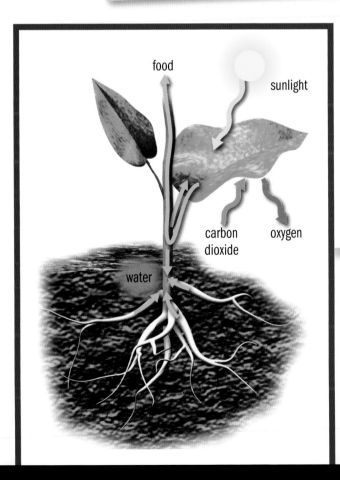

food

sunlight

carbon dioxide

oxygen

water

Leaves are the food factories of a plant.

WORD BANK
photosynthesis process plants use to make food using light energy from the sun
chlorophyll green-colored chemical that plays a key part in the process of photosynthesis

Producers in the water

The biggest primary producers in the water are plant-like creatures called **phytoplankton**. Most phytoplankton are very tiny—too small to see without a microscope. However, in some parts of the ocean they grow in such huge numbers that they change the color of the water. These large patches of phytoplankton can be seen from space.

Many of the plant-like creatures among the phytoplankton are **algae**. But there are also some larger kinds of algae, such as seaweed. Seaweed can grow very large. One kind of seaweed, known as giant kelp, can grow to 130 feet (40 meters) or more in length.

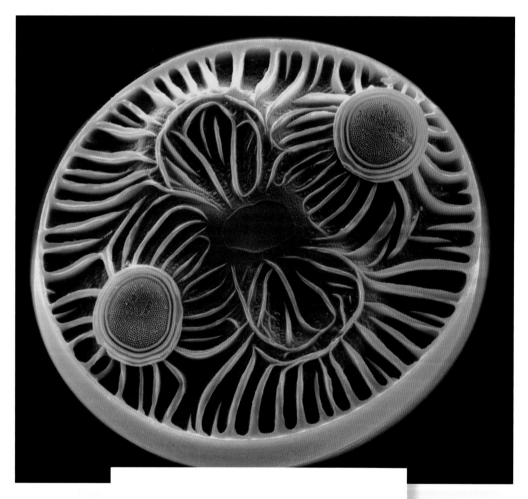

Diatoms like this one make up a large part of the phytoplankton. They are microscopic organisms and have a hard outer skeleton etched with complex patterns.

Unusual producers

In a few places on Earth there are producers that can make their own food without using energy from sunlight. Far beneath the ocean surface, for example, there are deep cracks in the ocean floor called hydrothermal vents. The rocks deep in these cracks are very hot. The heat comes originally from the center of the Earth, where nuclear reactions make the rocks hotter than the surface of the sun.

The hot rocks heat up the seawater, which then gushes up out of the vent. The hot water coming out of the vent is rich in dissolved chemicals. Some **microorganisms** are able to produce their own food using energy and chemicals from this hot water.

Another dark place where microorganisms produce their own food is deep inside some caves, where there is no sunlight, and the air is full of the smell of rotten eggs. These caves are home to strange bacteria called snottites (this really is their name). Huge numbers of snottites hang from the roof of the cave in long, white, gummy strings. They are able to produce energy from the chemicals that smell like rotten eggs and use it to make their own food.

Killer plants

Some plants live in soils that are very poor in nutrients such as nitrates. Without small amounts of these nutrients, the plants cannot survive. Instead of getting the nutrients from the soil, the plants get them by capturing and "eating" animals! The pitcher plant, for example, has leaves that form a deep, steep-sided cup. Insects that fall into the cup cannot get out again. A liquid in the bottom of the cup dissolves the insect's body, so that the plant can absorb its nutrients.

The Venus flytrap catches flies and other insects in its green, spiky "jaws." It then dissolves their bodies to get nutrients.

Consumers

Consumers are living things that eat other living things to get food.

Primary consumers

Primary consumers are plant-eaters. Grazers such as cows, sheep, zebras, and wildebeest live entirely on grass and other grassland plants. Browsers eat the leaves from bushes and trees. For example, giraffes use their long, strong tongues to pluck leaves from thorn trees.

Other plant-eaters feed on different parts of plants. Sparrows, larks, and many finches are seed-eaters. Toucans, parrots, flying foxes (a type of bat), and orangutans are all fruit-eaters. Insects such as aphids (greenfly) and leafhoppers suck plant sap, while butterflies and bees suck the nectar from flowers. A few animals, such as termites and bark beetles, eat wood.

Secondary consumers

Secondary consumers are animals that eat primary consumers. Many secondary consumers are **predators**—animals that hunt other animals for food. The animals that they hunt are called their **prey**. The most obvious predators are fierce killers such as lions and tigers, polar bears, crocodiles, sharks, eagles, and snakes. However, many other animals are also predators. They include insect hunters such as ants, wasps, and dragonflies, most spiders, scorpions, many frogs, monitor lizards, and small mammals such as weasels and otters.

Leaf miners are the **larvae** of some kinds of moth. These tiny maggots chomp their way through leaves from the inside, leaving tracks like those shown in this photo.

The hunters

Predators hunt their prey in different ways. Some chase their prey. Animals such as cheetahs are sprinters. They are very fast and try to catch their prey in a short chase. However, they cannot run for long, so if they judge the chase incorrectly, the prey may escape. Wolves and hunting dogs are long-distance chasers. Often they cannot run as fast as their prey, but they can keep going for hours. Eventually, the animal they are chasing becomes too tired to run any farther.

Big cats, such as leopards and tigers, are very good at **stalking** their prey. They move slowly and silently until they are close enough to leap out and take their victim by surprise. Jumping spiders are also good stalkers. They often spend several minutes moving slowly and carefully toward their prey before making a final leap.

Camouflage

Many predators rely on camouflage to help them surprise their prey. For example, some praying mantises are elaborately disguised to look like flowers, while a puff adder, a kind of viper, has camouflage markings that make it almost invisible on the forest floor.

Chameleons are "sit-and-wait" predators who are masters of disguise. Their skin can change color and pattern to blend in almost perfectly with their surroundings.

Other consumers

A few animals are **tertiary consumers**. This means they eat animals that eat other animals. Some insect-eaters, for example, may eat predatory insects. In the ocean, top predators can even be **quaternary consumers** (four steps removed from the producers). For example, a large ocean predator such as a shark or killer whale may eat large fish, which in turn feed on smaller fish. The smaller fish eat zooplankton (microscopic sea animals), and the zooplankton feed on **phytoplankton**.

These copper sharks are feeding on a school of sardines. The sardines eat zooplankton, and these in turn eat phytoplankton. This means this kind of shark is a tertiary consumer.

Many kinds of animal are omnivores—they eat both animals and plants for food. Brown and black bears, for example, eat foods such as fruit, fish, deer, and honey. Foxes and raccoons eat rabbits, mice, worms, fruit, and food waste from trash cans. Omnivores are both primary and secondary consumers.

Energy from food

Once food is in the body, we have to get energy from it. All living things, from the simplest **bacteria** to the largest whale, do this in the same way. They use a chemical process called **respiration**.

When you burn a fuel, it produces a lot of heat (and some light) in a short burst of energy. Most fuels contain the element carbon. When they burn, the carbon combines with oxygen from the air to make **carbon dioxide (CO_2)**.

The overall process of respiration is the same as for burning. The fuel (a sugar) is broken down to CO_2 plus water. However, instead of producing one big burst of energy, respiration breaks down sugars in a series of small steps. This makes it possible to capture some of the energy from the process in a useful way, instead of it all being turned into heat.

Respiration is also the "mirror image" of **photosynthesis**. In photosynthesis, plants turn water and CO_2 into sugars. Respiration does the reverse, turning sugars into CO_2 and water. Each process depends on the other for its fuel. Together, they make a sustainable cycle.

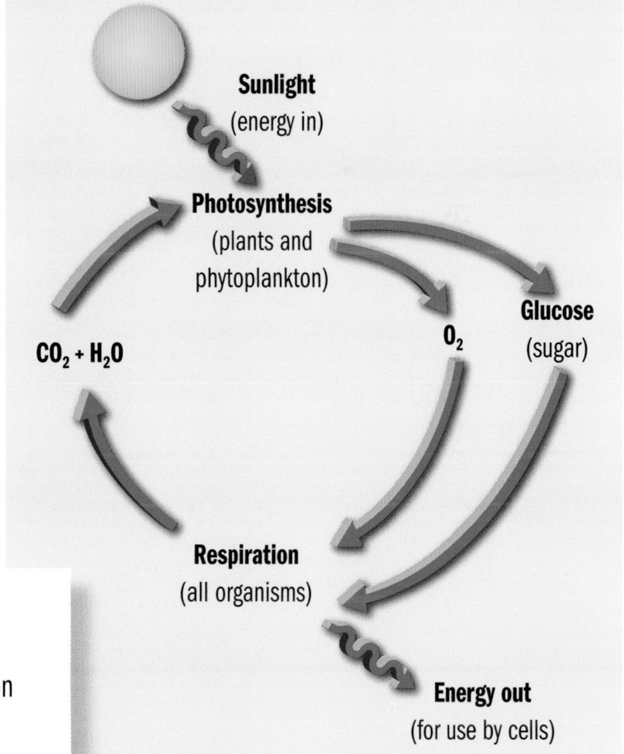

Sunlight
(energy in)

Photosynthesis
(plants and phytoplankton)

Glucose
(sugar)

O_2

CO_2 + H_2O

Respiration
(all organisms)

Energy out
(for use by cells)

This diagram shows how photosynthesis and respiration are related.

Plant-eaters versus meat-eaters

For most herbivores (plant-eating animals), food is easy to find. Plants do not run away when an animal wants to eat them. However, plants do have ways to avoid being eaten. Many of them contain tough substances such as **cellulose** and **lignin**, which animals cannot **digest**. Other plants make toxins (poisonous chemicals) that can kill an animal trying to eat them.

The long thorns on this acacia tree are an effective defense against many animals.

Some animals get around plant defenses often with help from **microbes**, or tiny living things, or viruses, that can only be seen under a microscope. For example, cows and sheep have an extra stomach called the rumen. It contains billions of bacteria that can break down cellulose. Termites eat an even tougher plant food —wood. Their guts contain a special microbe that is able to break down lignin.

Other plant-eaters have no helpers to break down the tough parts of plants. They simply have to eat huge numbers of plants in order to get enough nutrition.

Animal flesh (meat) is much more nutritious than plant food. The **nutrients** in meat are suitable for other animals and are easier to digest. However, eating animal food has its disadvantages. Most animals do not wait around to be eaten—they run away from predators. Chasing other animals, or even stalking them or lying in wait, uses more energy than finding plants to eat.

WHAT IT MEANS FOR US

We sometimes talk about goats or pigs as animals that will "eat anything." But humans eat a really enormous range of foods. The kinds of meat eaten around the world by humans include insects, snails, frogs, snakes, birds, and almost any kind of mammal. We also eat many different parts of plants, including the roots (for example, carrots and potatoes), stems (rhubarb and celery), leaves (spinach, lettuce, and cabbage), flowers (cauliflower and artichokes), seeds, nuts, and of course, all kinds of fruit.

A Simple Food Chain

At the simplest level, a food chain connects a primary producer, a primary consumer, and a secondary consumer. For example, in a meadow or grassland, the main primary producers are grasses. Mice living in grassland rely on the grasses and grass seeds for their food. And mice are a major food for snakes living in grassland.

Connections in the chain

All the living things in a food chain are connected. Changes in any one link in the chain will affect the others. For example, suppose there is a **drought**, and the grasses dry up. There will be far less food for mice, and many of them will die. This obviously affects the mouse population, but it also affects snakes. Fewer mice means less food for the snakes, so many snakes will also probably die.

Common confusions

Who's eating whom?

In diagrams that show food chains, people can get confused about which direction the arrows are pointing. In diagrams of this type, the arrow always points towards the **species** that is doing the eating. One way to remember this is to think of the arrows as shorthand for "is eaten by...." The arrow also shows the flow of energy from one group to the next (see page 20).

This is a simple food chain.

grass and seeds   mouse   snake   hawk

If the numbers of mice or snakes fell for some reason, this would have a different effect. For example, suppose another animal comes into the food chain—a large hawk or eagle that feeds on snakes. If the hawk is a successful hunter, the snake population may begin to decrease. Fewer snakes means that fewer mice get eaten—more survive. As mice numbers grow, they eat more grass and seeds, and this could have an effect on the grassland itself.

These examples show how changes affect more than just one living thing—they affect the whole food chain. In a real environment, things are even more complicated. Read on to find out why.

Top of the heap

An animal at the top of a food chain is usually what is known as a top **predator**. A top predator in a rainforest might be a tiger, a crocodile, or a harpy eagle such as the one below.

This food chain shows the feeding relationships between living things in a freshwater river or lake.

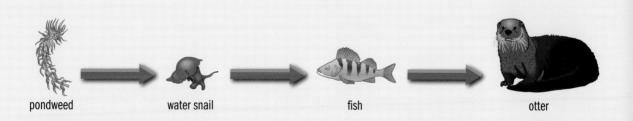

pondweed → water snail → fish → otter

From Chains to Webs

In a real environment, there is no such thing as a simple **food chain**. There are many other connections that complicate the situation.

Changing diets

Most animals do not eat just one kind of food. A snake might eat frogs, young birds, large insects, and eggs, as well as mice. A hawk might hunt other birds as well as snakes. A mouse might feed on berries and fruit as well as grass and seeds.

If an animal eats several kinds of food, it can change its diet if one kind of food is scarce. For example, suppose that there are not many mice for a grassland snake to eat. It might make up for this by eating more frogs or more birds' eggs. Changing the diet this way may help an animal to survive when conditions are tough. It also means that the animal is part of several different food chains, not just one.

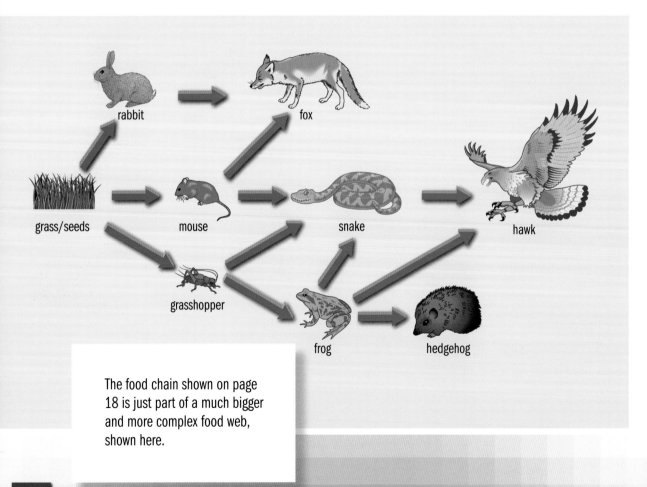

The food chain shown on page 18 is just part of a much bigger and more complex food web, shown here.

Competition

If a food is good to eat and widely available, several different **species** may eat it. For example, the grasses in a grassland area are food for a whole range of different animals, from cattle to insects. Grass is widely available, so many animals can feed on it without a problem. But some kinds of food are not so widely available. For instance, snakes are not the only animals that eat mice. Weasels and falcons also eat them.

These three animal species compete for limited supplies of the same food. Often one species will come out ahead in the competition. The other species may fall in numbers, or they may survive in other ways. They might switch to other types of food, or move to an area where there is less competition.

Arctic and red foxes

Different species may win the competition in different environments. For example, Arctic foxes live in the Arctic areas of Russia and North America. Their thick fur keeps them warm in freezing temperatures. They are also quite small, which means they do not need very much food to survive.

Further south in Europe, Asia, and North America, red foxes are the main fox species. They are bigger than Arctic foxes. Where both species live together, the red foxes chase the Arctic foxes away from the best dens and feeding areas. The Arctic foxes can only compete in places where it is very cold, and food is scarce.

As winters have gotten warmer, red foxes, such as the one shown here, have pushed Arctic foxes further north.

Finding a niche

Often species can avoid direct competition by living in slightly different places or by eating slightly different foods. One example is the feeding habits of birds that live along seashores, such as curlews and plovers. Different species of shore bird manage to avoid direct competition by feeding in different places. For example, some species feed in deeper water than others. Birds also have beaks of different lengths and shapes. These different beaks have evolved (developed gradually) over time as birds have become adapted to feed in particular ways.

Avoiding competition

When male and female birds are raising their young, both parents have to find food in the same area. Sparrow hawks avoid feeding competition by growing to different sizes. The male is smaller than the female, and hunts smaller **prey**. This means that the two birds do not compete for the same food.

In these and other situations, each species living in a **habitat** adapts to a particular way of life and of feeding. This is known as the species' **ecological niche**. If a species cannot find its own ecological niche, the chances are that it will die out.

Different shore bird species have different feeding habits. By feeding at different depths and in different ways, they avoid direct competition.

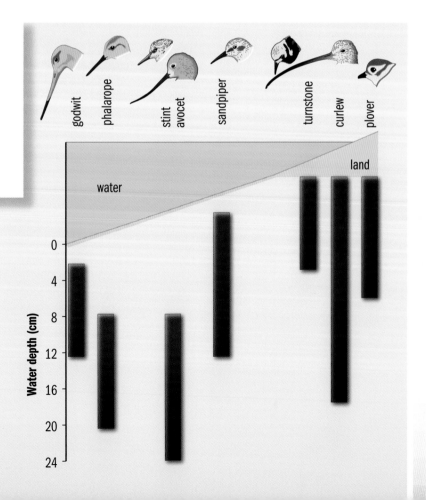

Food on the move

Some species survive in places where there is limited food by staying in one place for a short time and then moving on. Many bird species spend the winter in warm climates and then **migrate** to cooler places in the summer. The long journey is worthwhile because their summer home has a plentiful food supply for feeding their young.

A web of connections

In a particular habitat, there are many different food chains. The chains are connected together in many different ways in a complex web. In all but the simplest habitats, this web of connections is very complex. This makes it difficult to predict what will happen if something changes. If one connection in a **food web** changes or is broken, it can affect many other living things in the web.

Sea otters and kelp

Sea otters live in areas where giant seaweed, called kelp, form huge underwater "forests." These kelp forests are a rich habitat for many other living things. One of the sea otter's foods is sea urchins, animals that eat kelp.

In many areas, the population of sea otters has been reduced by over-hunting. Where there are few sea otters, the number of sea urchins increases. Where this happens, the kelp forest can be destroyed.

Sea otters help to maintain the rich kelp forest habitat.

Common confusions

Greedy predators?

In a food web, the top **predators** do not eat all the other consumers. Each predator eats only a small number of species.

WORD BANK
habitat environment in which a species of organism lives
ecological niche way of living and feeding within a habitat that allows a particular species

Food Pyramids

An apple is a good food because the carbohydrates and other **nutrients** in the apple are stores of energy. This stored energy is captured from the sun during **photosynthesis** (see pages 8–9 and 15).

Energy losses

When we eat an apple, our bodies are able to use some of the energy from it. This energy helps us to move around, breathe, and grow. However, we can only use some of the apple's energy. A lot of it is lost as waste.

There is a large loss of energy at every stage in a **food chain**. Plants can only capture a small part of the sun's energy. Animals can only make use of a small part of the energy in their foods. At each stage, energy is lost as waste. On average, only about 10 percent of the food that an animal eats is turned into **biomass** (living tissues such as skin, muscle, and hair).

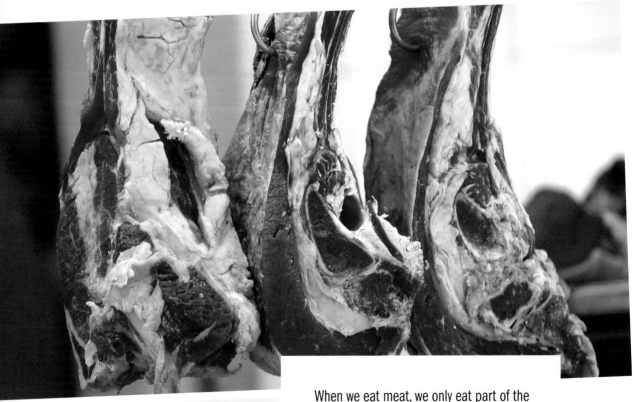

When we eat meat, we only eat part of the animal. We don't usually eat the head, skin, hooves, or fur, and we get useful energy from only part of what we do eat.

A biomass pyramid

We can use a diagram called a biomass pyramid to show how the amount of biomass changes as we go up the food chain. One such pyramid is shown below. Each section of the pyramid shows a **trophic level** for one type of producer or consumer. The bottom section shows the biomass of all the primary producers in an area. For example, it could show the biomass of all the plants in a forest.

The second section of the pyramid shows the biomass of all the primary consumers (plant-eaters). This is much less than the biomass of the producers for two reasons. First, the consumers only eat about 20 percent of all the plants available. Second, we have seen that only a small amount of the plant food that the consumers eat is turned into biomass. In this pyramid, only 5 percent of the forest plants are turned into biomass.

The top section of the pyramid is the biomass of the secondary consumers (the predators). The secondary consumers only eat about 20 percent of all the plant-eaters in the forest. About 15 percent of what they eat is turned into biomass.

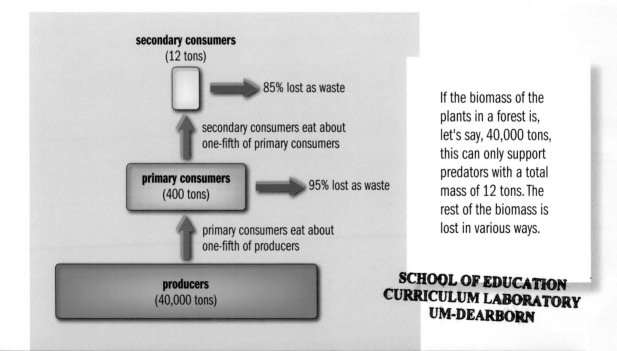

If the biomass of the plants in a forest is, let's say, 40,000 tons, this can only support predators with a total mass of 12 tons. The rest of the biomass is lost in various ways.

WORD BANK
biomass   dry weight of living material
trophic level level in which the consumers are the same number of steps away from the producers

Numbers, biomass, and energy

Instead of showing biomass, a pyramid can be used to show the numbers of living things at each trophic level, or how much energy is held at each level.

The three pyramids below are all for the same woodland habitat. The pyramid of energy is similar to the biomass pyramid. As you move up the trophic levels, less and less energy or biomass is available. However, the pyramid of numbers is different. There are fewer primary producers than primary consumers! This is because the primary producers are trees. One tree can feed thousands of plant-eating insects.

These are the pyramids of biomass, energy, and numbers for a mixed-oak woodland.

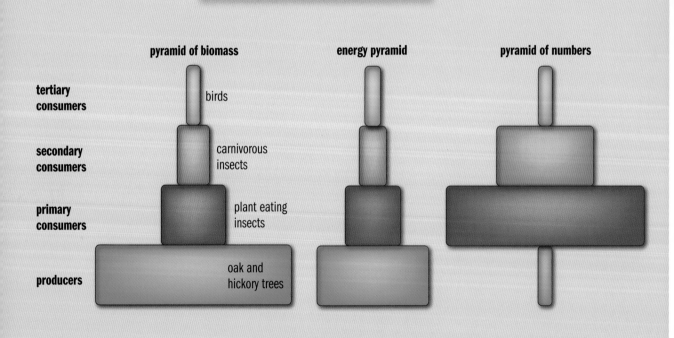

| pyramid of biomass | energy pyramid | pyramid of numbers |

tertiary consumers — birds

secondary consumers — carnivorous insects

primary consumers — plant eating insects

producers — oak and hickory trees

WHAT IT MEANS FOR US

Overall, it probably would be more energy-efficient to eat more vegetables and less meat. It takes 15,400–30,800 pounds (7–14 metric tons) of plant food to produce an average-sized cow weighing about 1,540 pounds (700 kilograms). And that's not the end of the story. We only eat about half of the weight of a live cow. So 15,400–30,800 pounds (7–14 metric tons) of plant food produces only about 770 pounds (350 kilograms) of meat.

These numbers suggest that we would get much more food from farms by growing crops rather than by raising animals for meat. However, it's not quite that simple. When we grow a field of wheat, for example, we do not eat the whole crop. We use the seeds (usually to make flour) and throw the rest away. Also, plant food is not so easy to **digest** as animal food. It often contains large amounts of roughage (things that we cannot digest, which become waste). Finally, animals such as sheep can be raised on rough pasture that is no good for growing crops.

Should we all be vegetarians?

It takes 1,000,000 units of energy from sunlight to produce every 100 units of energy a lion gets from its food.

Using Up the Waste

Food pyramids show that only a small amount of the energy from food is turned into **biomass**. What happens to the rest? Some of it becomes heat. This is especially true for **endothermic** (warm-blooded) animals, such as mammals and birds. They use some of the energy from food to generate heat. This helps to keep their bodies warm even in cold weather. Some of the energy is used for moving around. But quite a lot of the food animals eat ends up as waste—urine and dung. A third waste product is the gas **carbon dioxide (CO_2)**. This is the waste product from **respiration** (see page 15).

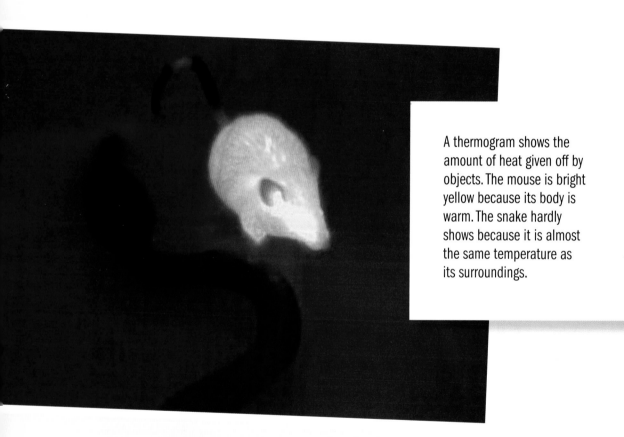

A thermogram shows the amount of heat given off by objects. The mouse is bright yellow because its body is warm. The snake hardly shows because it is almost the same temperature as its surroundings.

Living on waste

Many living things have adapted to survive on the waste products of other animals or plants. These kinds of animals are called **detritus** feeders.

Detritus is not just urine and dung. It also includes dead plants and plant parts—for example, the dead leaves from trees. Dead animals or animal remains are also detritus.

There are whole groups of **organisms** that specialize in feeding on waste. Larger detritus feeders include beetles, flies, snails, and earthworms. Termites are detritus feeders that eat the leaf litter on the floor of a forest, and help to break up the dead leaves.

Detritus

In the sea and in freshwater, waste material falls to the riverbed or ocean floor, where it provides food for many **species**. In freshwater streams, detritus is often the base of the food system, rather than living plants. Dead leaves and other parts of plants drop into the stream from plants growing on the banks, or in shallow water. As it breaks down, this detritus turns into a rich food that is eaten by small primary consumers, such as water snails. These then become food for fish and other secondary consumers.

Dung beetles are the clean-up squad of the animal world. They feed mainly on animal dung. They also roll dung into balls and bury it as a food supply for their young.

Decomposers

Detritus feeders are only the first stage of breaking down animal and plant waste. Another group of organisms, mainly **bacteria** and **fungi**, take the process a stage further. They are "rotters", or decomposers. Fungi are very important decomposers, especially for rotting wood. Fungi include mushrooms and molds.

The main "body" of a fungus is not the small part we see—the mushroom or mold. It is a mass of very tiny threads called hyphae. These spread all through the material that the fungus is growing on. The hyphae break down the material and absorb **nutrients** from it.

Full circle

Bacteria and fungi decompose animal and plant waste into very simple substances. On land, these simple chemicals may be released into the air or become part of the soil. Then they can be soaked up by plants once again as they make new foods. In the oceans, the nutrients enrich the water, and help **phytoplankton** to grow. The nutrients that were first used by producers to make their food have come full circle and enter the food chain again.

Insect clocks

Forensic scientists have done many studies on how human corpses rot. When a dead body is left out in the open, insects and other creatures are quickly attracted to it. As the body changes and decomposes, different insects come to feed. In the early stages of decay, fly **larvae** are most common. In later stages of decay, there are large numbers of adult beetles. Eventually, when the body dries out, centipedes, woodlice, and cockroaches arrive.

By examining which insects are living on a corpse, scientists can tell roughly how long the body has been dead.

These fungi are growing on a dead tree. The main part of the fungus is not the mushrooms we see, but the thread-like hyphae inside the wood.

This diagram shows how decomposers fit into a food chain.

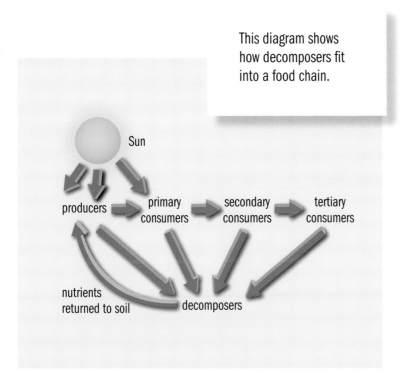

Recycling waste

Mudflats are areas of mud on a coast or a river that are uncovered at low tide. Some kinds of shellfish feed on the waste from other animals that collects on the mud surface. But the shellfish do not feed on the waste itself. They wait until decomposing bacteria and other **microbes** grow all over the waste. The shellfish then eat the decomposing waste. Most of the nutrition is in the microbes that cover the waste.

Antarctic Food Web

The Antarctic continent is a huge, freezing, empty wilderness covered in ice. Hardly any living things can survive at the heart of the continent, but on the coasts it is different. The sea around the Antarctic is full of life. This makes it possible for animals to live on land and get food from the sea.

A simple food web

There are many different animal and plant **species** in the Antarctic. But there are far fewer different species than in other parts of the world. This means that scientists have been able to understand more about the **food web** of the Antarctic than of any other **habitat**.

Important shrimps

At the center of the Antarctic food web are small, shrimp-like animals called krill. The water of the Antarctic Ocean is rich in **nutrients.** This means that the ocean can feed huge numbers of krill. The krill are primary consumers. In the summer, they feed on **phytoplankton**, which grow in huge numbers. In winter, pack ice forms on the ocean surface. Above, on the surface of the ice, temperatures fall to –22 °F (–30 °C) or even less. Freezing winds make it feel even colder. But under the pack ice, the water never gets colder than about 28 °F (–2 °C), so winter conditions in the water are not too harsh. Many living things have adapted to live in this environment.

During the Antarctic winter, it is dark most of the time. However, as light begins to return in the spring, microscopic, plant-like ice **algae** begin to grow on the underside of the pack ice. The krill feed on them, swimming upside down and vacuuming them up.

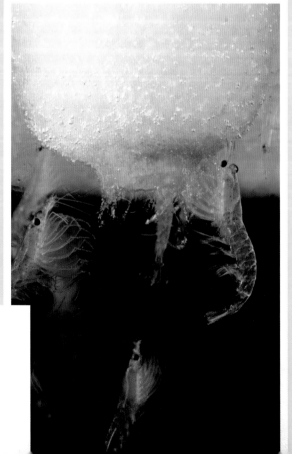

One krill can scrape off the algae from a square foot of sea ice in just 10 minutes. Imagine what 600,000 billion can do!

The krill spend the whole winter eating and growing. By the time the pack ice melts, there are huge numbers of them. There can be as many as 600,000 billion krill, weighing over 50 million tons. They are the most abundant animals on the planet.

Antarctic endotherms and ectotherms

Most the top predators in the Antarctic are either mammals or birds. Both of these groups are endothermic. However, a few large Antarctic predators are ectotherms, for example giant squid and sleeper sharks. They have adapted to be able to keep their bodies working in the freezing Antarctic waters.

Leopard seals

Although leopard seals are top predators, they also feed directly on krill, especially in winter. They have three-pronged molar (back) teeth similar to those of the crabeater seal, which eats mainly krill. The teeth act as an efficient krill sieve.

A simplified version of the Antarctic food web. The different-colored arrows indicate different **trophic levels**.

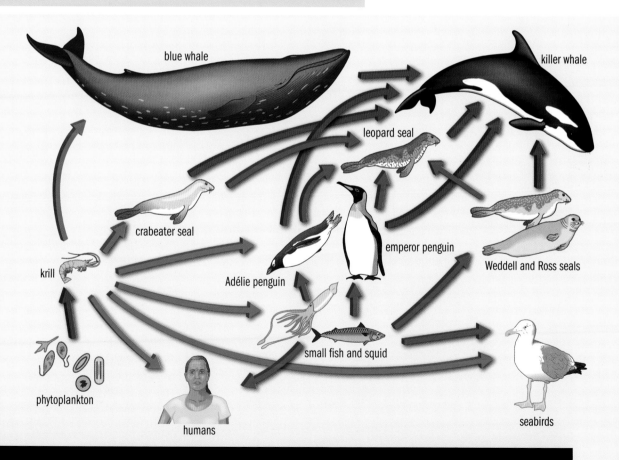

blue whale · killer whale · leopard seal · crabeater seal · emperor penguin · Weddell and Ross seals · krill · Adélie penguin · small fish and squid · phytoplankton · seabirds · humans

Feeding frenzy

The huge numbers of krill provide food for many other animals during the Antarctic summer. Some species eat almost nothing else. Crabeater seals, for example, are incorrectly named because they do not eat crabs. Their diet is almost entirely krill. Other animals that eat large amounts of krill include many fish species, penguins, and huge **baleen whales**. Krill-eating fish provide food for larger fish, penguins, some seals, and killer whales. Humans catch fish in the Antarctic Ocean, and we also catch krill directly.

Instead of teeth, whales like this one have large plates made of a stiff material called baleen. The baleen plates act as a sieve, or strainer. They filter small animals out of the water but let the water itself pass through.

There are three top predators in the Arctic Ocean. Most dangerous are killer whales, or orcas. They hunt seals, penguins, and sometimes even young whales. Often they hunt in small groups, called pods. Leopard seals are fierce solo hunters. They prowl mainly in shallow waters, looking for penguins and smaller seals. Southern elephant seals are the biggest of all seals. They are deep-sea divers. They hunt at depths of 3,300 feet (1,000 meters) or more for squid and fish.

Keystone species

Research has shown that krill are central to the Antarctic food web. Any changes in krill populations can have large effects on other species in the web. The krill are what is known as a keystone species in the Antarctic. Keystone species are animals or plants that are very important in a particular habitat. They are called keystone species because they act rather like the keystone of an arch. The keystone is the central stone at the top of an arch. If the keystone is removed, the arch collapses.

Scientists have identified keystone species in other environments. In some tropical forests in South America, fig trees and a few others act as keystone species. These trees produce fruit throughout the year and provide food that is vital for many mammals and birds. A species of starfish is a keystone species along rocky shores of northwest North America. This predatory starfish feeds mainly on mussels. When the starfish is removed from the habitat, the mussel populations take over and cover the shores so completely that they force out most other species.

Constantly Changing

Habitats change all the time. Extreme weather can cause floods, droughts, or forest fires. New species may arrive in a habitat from another area. And humans have had a large effect on some habitats. Whenever changes happen, food relationships change, too.

Natural changes

The weather is the cause of many natural changes that affect feeding relationships. For example, small changes in the weather can lead to a huge crop of fruit in one year, but a poor fruit crop another year. In a poor year, many fruit-eating birds may not be able to feed their young. The result could be that, in the next year, there is a smaller bird population.

Changes caused by humans

Today, many of the most dramatic changes in feeding relationships are caused by human activity. An example of this is the effect that fishing has had on the Great Barrier Reef in Australia. This is one of the biggest **coral reefs** in the world. Thousands of different species live on the reefs. However, overfishing has caused problems.

For example, fishing boats catch large numbers of groupers, which are good to eat. Groupers are **predators** that feed mainly on damselfish. When grouper numbers fall, more damselfish survive. However, this is a problem for the coral. Damselfish clear small patches of coral so that the **algae** that they like to eat can grow. When damselfish numbers get too large, too much coral is cleared, and the reef is taken over by algae.

Shrinking habitats

Some human activities have much wider effects than over-hunting. Building towns and cities, or clearing land for farming, damages or destroys habitats. Often a large natural habitat can become broken up into several small patches. As areas of a natural habitat shrink, it can reach the stage where there is no longer enough **biomass** in the area to support top predators (see the biomass pyramid on page 25). The predators cannot find enough food or mates, and eventually they die out.

WHAT IT MEANS FOR US

In the more developed countries, we rely on a complex artificial web of connections to supply our food. We transport food from all parts of the world to reach us while it is still fresh. As in the natural **food web**, changes to one of the connections in the web has wide-ranging effects. For example, in the summer of 2010, a severe drought damaged the wheat harvest in Russia. Then, in late 2010 and early 2011, the wheat harvest in Australia was damaged by floods. These two events affected the price of wheat worldwide. The cost of bread, breakfast cereal, and many other foods went up.

Bluefin tuna are a very popular food in Japan. Because of overfishing, the species is close to extinction.

Global changes

Feeding connections between living things are not limited to a particular area. Species such as whales, sea turtles, and some birds travel great distances each year. Green turtles, for example, breed on islands in Hawaii and then travel to feeding grounds as far away as Japan. Species, such as the green turtle, connect **food chains** across the world.

These global connections can have far-reaching effects. Pollution has probably caused the most damage to food chains and webs worldwide. A particular problem is chemical **pollutants** that remain in the body—ones that are not flushed out in the urine. These kinds of chemicals can build up in the food chain.

DDT

To understand the snowball effects of pollutants, let's consider a chemical called DDT. In the past this was sprayed on crops to stop pests from eating them. In small doses DDT does not hurt large animals, but in larger doses it can be toxic.

When primary consumers ate plants sprayed with DDT, the chemical gradually built up in their bodies. Predators that ate primary consumers containing DDT got much larger doses of the chemical. This was because each animal they ate had already stored DDT in its body. At each step in the food chain, the amount of DDT grew. Global connections between food webs also meant that DDT spread across the world. It was even found in polar bears in the Arctic.

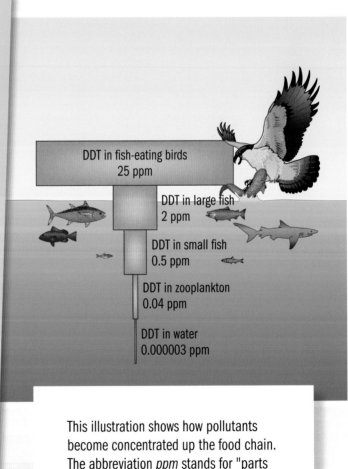

DDT in fish-eating birds
25 ppm

DDT in large fish
2 ppm

DDT in small fish
0.5 ppm

DDT in zooplankton
0.04 ppm

DDT in water
0.000003 ppm

This illustration shows how pollutants become concentrated up the food chain. The abbreviation *ppm* stands for "parts per million." So, the larger the number, the greater the amount of DDT there is.

Ups and downs

Changes in the availability of food can make the populations of some animals go up and down in a regular cycle. An example is the snowshoe hare, a herbivore that lives in northern North America. The population of the snowshoe hare goes up and down over a cycle of 8 to 11 years. In years when there is plenty of plant food, hare numbers grow rapidly. But eventually there are so many hares that the habitat cannot support them. As a result, the number of hares drops dramatically.

Changes in the snowshoe hare population also affect their main predator, the lynx. As hare populations grow, lynx populations grow, too. Then, as the hare numbers drop, the lynx lose their main food. They switch to eating other prey, such as mice. However, the number of mice cannot support the large lynx population, and the number of lynx also drops.

Snowshoe hares are the main prey for lynx.

Conclusion

We often hear on the news that a **species** of insect or a plant that we have never heard of is in danger of dying out. Often people think, "Does it matter?" An understanding of **food chains** and webs helps us to realize that such a loss can matter very much. As we have seen, the loss of a species can have an effect across the food web. It could even affect **food webs** far away.

There are over 35,000 different species of this kind of moth. If one species died out, would it really matter?

Biodiversity

We saw in the Antarctic food web that a **habitat** with small numbers of species is **fragile**. In a habitat with few species, changes in one link in the food web can have a large effect. In richer habitats, where there are thousands of different species, changes to one link in the web are likely to have less of an effect.

Biodiversity is a measure of the numbers of different animals and plants living in an area. When there is a large variety of life, biodiversity is high. When a habitat has few species, biodiversity is low.

All over the world, humans are changing habitats through pollution, clearing of land, and hunting and fishing. The general effect of these changes is to reduce biodiversity. The more that biodiversity decreases, the more likely it is that the loss of an obscure species from the food web will have an effect on human lives.

WHAT IT MEANS FOR US

In the 1990s, the numbers of white-backed vultures in southern Asia began to fall dramatically. Over ten years the population fell by 99.9 percent. The fall was caused by a drug called diclofenac that was given to cows as a painkiller. When the cows were killed, the vultures fed on their remains, and the drug got into their bodies. Thousands of vultures died because the drug was a poison for them.

Before their numbers fell, vultures were important for helping clean up human garbage and waste in southern Asia. As the vultures died out, large packs of feral dogs (dogs that have turned wild) began to take their place. These dogs carry the disease rabies, which can infect humans. The increasingly large numbers of dogs have also attracted leopard **predators**, which sometimes attack and kill children.

White-backed vultures are scavengers (they eat leftovers and waste). Until their numbers fell, they were an important "clean-up squad" in many Asian cities.

Forest and Desert Food Webs

A forest food web

Oak trees are important **species** in many North American forests. In the autumn, acorns are the main food source for huge numbers of primary consumers—from insects to black bears. The smaller primary consumers provide food for secondary consumers such as foxes, coyotes, and cougars. In the spring and summer, when there are no acorns or other fruits, bears become **predators**, too. They may eat anything from insects to deer, and even moose.

In an oak forest, the "pyramid" of numbers is kite-shaped (see artwork below). A few trees provide food for thousands of primary consumers, such as insects and birds. The primary consumers provide food for hundreds of secondary consumers. However, if we look at the **biomass**, or the amount of energy in the **habitat**, we find that there is much more energy stored in the trees than in the primary or secondary consumers.

The food web for a North American forest.

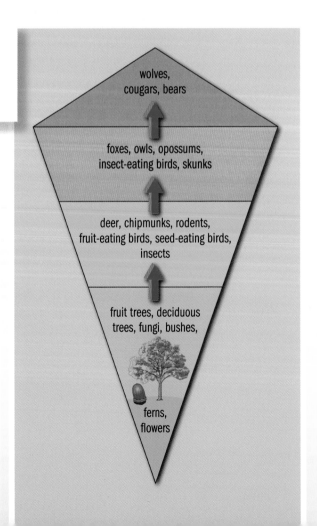

wolves, cougars, bears

foxes, owls, opossums, insect-eating birds, skunks

deer, chipmunks, rodents, fruit-eating birds, seed-eating birds, insects

fruit trees, deciduous trees, fungi, bushes,

ferns, flowers

A desert food web

Deserts are very dry, so plants find it hard to grow. There are far fewer plants than in the forest, and they have far less biomass. Because plants are so scarce, there are not many animals either. In the driest deserts, most primary consumers are **ectothermic** animals, such as insects and lizards. They need less energy to stay alive, so they survive better where food is scarce. Most secondary consumers (for example, snakes and large lizards) are also **ectothermic.**

In less dry deserts, some large mammals find ways to survive. Camels survive in the desert by storing fat in their humps. When they are thirsty, their bodies can extract water from this fat store. Animals such as springboks, oryx, and even elephants can survive in the Namib Desert. This is because on some mornings thick fogs form along the desert coast. The fog leaves moisture on the plants, which the animals can drink.

A desert food web is simpler than a forest web because fewer species live in deserts.

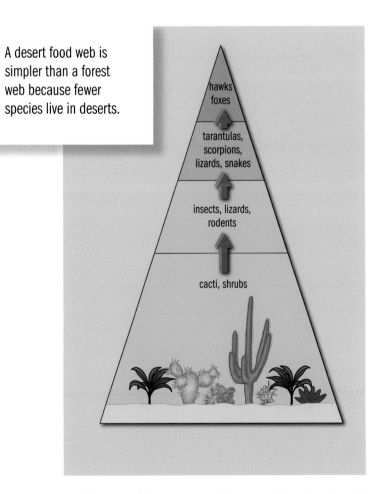

hawks
foxes

tarantulas,
scorpions,
lizards, snakes

insects, lizards,
rodents

cacti, shrubs

Glossary

algae group of plant-like living things that live mainly in water. Many algae are microscopic, but some, such as seaweed, are larger.

bacteria (singular: **bacterium**) single-celled living things

baleen whale large whale that has, rather than teeth in its mouth, structures made from a horny material called baleen

biomass dry weight of living material

carbon dioxide (CO_2) gas in the air that plants can use to make sugars for food

cell tiny building block that all living things are made from

cellulose carbohydrate (chemical made from long chains of sugar molecules) that is important in plant cell walls. Cellulose forms strong fibers that are used to help build plant parts.

chlorophyll green-colored chemical that plays a key part in the process of photosynthesis

coral reef rich habitat found mainly in shallow seas, based on animals called coral. Coral grow like plants and have a strong outer case made from limestone.

detritus waste from other animals or plants

digest break food down into simpler substances that can be absorbed into the body

drought long period without rainfall

ecological niche way of living and feeding within a habitat that allows a particular species to obtain food and survive

ectothermic needs to get heat from the surroundings to keep warm

endothermic produces heat within the body to keep temperature constant, no matter how the temperature of the environment changes

food chain group of organisms that are connected through what they eat: organism 1 eats organism 2, which eats organism 3, and so on

food web group of organisms that are connected together through feeding relationships in a network, or web, rather than a single chain

fungus (plural: **fungi**) one of the group of living things that includes mushrooms, toadstools, and molds. Many fungi are decomposers.

fragile easily broken or damaged

gene section of DNA inside living cells that passes on characteristics from one generation to the next

habitat environment in which a species or organism lives

hibernate sleep deeply through the winter months to save energy

larva (plural: **larvae**) young animal that is significantly different from the adult (for example, a caterpillar or a maggot)

lignin tough, strong material produced in plants that is one of the main components of wood

microbe tiny living thing or virus that can only be seen under a microscope

microorganism tiny living thing that can only be seen under a microscope

migrate move from one area to another every year or season. Some species of living things migrate each year in order to find food.

nutrient chemical an organism needs to live and grow

organism any kind of living thing

photosynthesis process plants use to make food using light energy from the sun

phytoplankton microscopic living things found in the ocean that are able to photosynthesize like plants do

pollinate carry pollen from plant to plant so that they can reproduce. Pollination is usually done by insects or birds.

pollutant chemical in the environment that can cause illness or death in living things

predator animal that hunts other animals for food

prey animal that is hunted and eaten by a predator

quaternary consumer animal that eats tertiary consumers

respiration chemical process by which all organisms get energy from their food

scrubland area where the main plants are shrubs (woody plants that are smaller than trees)

species specific type of animal or plant, the members of which can breed together to produce young

stalk hunt by moving slowly and quietly, and staying hidden in order to get close to a prey animal

starch complex chemical made up of chains of sugars joined together. It is used as an energy store by most plants.

tertiary consumer animal that eats secondary consumers

trophic level one of the levels of a food web in which the organisms are the same number of steps away from the primary producers

Find Out More

Books

Kalman, Bobbie. *What Are Food Chains and Webs?* New York, NY: Crabtree Publishing, 2008.

O'Donnell, Liam. *The World of Food Chains with Max Axiom, Super Scientist* (Graphic Library: Graphic Science series). Mankato, MN: Capstone Press, 2007.

Rhodes, Mary Jo and David Hall. *Life in a Kelp Forest* (Undersea Encounters series). Danbury, CT: Children's Press, 2006.

Solway, Andrew. *Food Chains and Webs: The Struggle to Survive.* Vero Beach, FL: Rourke Publishing, 2007.

Spilsbury, Louise and Richard. *Food Chains and Webs* (Science Answers series). Chicago, IL: Heinemann Library, 2004.

Stille, Darlene Ruth. *Nature Interrupted: The Science of Environmental Chain Reactions* (Headline Science series). Mankato, MN: Compass Point Books, 2009.

Townsend, John. *Rotters!* (Fusion: Life Processes and Living Things series). Chicago, IL: Raintree, 2005.

Wallace, Holly. *Food Chains and Webs* (Life Processes series). Chicago, IL: Heinemann Library, 2007.

Websites

www.bbc.co.uk/schools/ks2bitesize/science/living_things/food_chains/play.shtml
Visit this website and click on Food Chains to find simple food chain activities.

www.discoveringantarctica.org.uk/multimedia/flash/4_eating.html
Discovering Antarctica: Who's Eating Whom? This website has information and activities based on the Antarctic food web.

www.field-studies-council.org/urbaneco/urbaneco/introduction/feeding.htm
Urban Ecosystems: Feeding Relationships. This website has information about food chains in towns and cities, from the Field Studies Council.

polardiscovery.whoi.edu/antarctica/ecosystem.html
Polar Discovery: Antarctica's Ecosystem. Use this website to learn more about food webs in Antarctica.

Topics to research

Temperature control

Find out more about endotherms and ectotherms. Mammals and birds are not the only animals that are endotherms. See if you can find out which other animals keep themselves warm in cold conditions. What about dinosaurs? Were they endotherms or ectotherms? Do scientists know?

Phytoplankton

We know a lot about plants—but what about the living things that are the main producers in the oceans? Where are good places to find phytoplankton? Can you find the names of three different kinds? A good place to start is in the Arctic or Antarctic. See, for example: nsidc.org/seaice/environment/phytoplankton.html

Parasites

Parasites are an interesting part of the food web. Can you find out about common human parasites? What about parasites on other animals? For which animal is the Varroa mite a parasite?

Index